"Part dreamscape, part dirge, and all rapturous music, *REJOICER* adds another voice to the fierce tradition of American Surrealism. This book amasses so much lyrical invention and ardor that we come to see the world as a disembodied space as boundless as it is inescapable. A stunning work of art."

— Michael McGriff, author of *Eternal Sentences*

"Skyler Osborne seems surprised and amused by the sensorially overloaded modern world in his debut book of poems, but his *REJOICER* is painfully aware that 'There is no distance between the Lord/and his monsters tearing up the yard.' Osborne's surreal images navigate childhood and the cosmos with equal tenderness from a kaleidoscopic middle America scored with terrors, absurdities, and indignities. It's a world of 'Names of streets and songs/ and the family bowing backwards until they vanished, It all vanished. And it estranged memory—...' By torquing vestiges of memory into a new reality, a gentle poet de-fangs a hostile universe. Reader, the resilience of these fraught poems will inspire your broken spirit."

— Jane Miller, author of *The Greater Leisures*

"Here is an angel 'cashed out in the evergreens, an astonished child spreading its wings with a stick.' Here is a sleeping brain 'beaming like a car in a swimming pool' or cicadas 'rhyming on the willows.' In these lush and urgent poems, Skyler Osborne meditates on the complexities of religious and ritual imagination, on guilt and magic and the vagaries of memory. These are wonderful poems, rich in imagery and metaphor, always gesturing toward the unknowable and profound. *REJOICER* is a brilliant first book, surprising me at every turn. I will read it again with pleasure."

— Kevin Prufer, author of *Churches*

"In *REJOICER*, Skyler Osborne's first collection of poetry, we witness a speaker's struggle to find meaning, and even something approaching the divine, in our troubled times. Set in the Midwest, amid urban blight and a dark family history, the beautiful and the terrible are often impossible to disentangle: 'In the air where you have loved me/bees scatter like the Leonids/from the arms of boys/burning hives in the alley.' Osborne directs us to confront a human and natural world at odds in these visionary lyrics, as well as our own complicity in these destructive collisions. 'I know I've made a lot of mistakes,' the poet writes. 'Every day I stack rocks and forgive one thing.' Ultimately, these poems show us that empathy and forgiveness for the living, even with all our flaws, give us something worth rejoicing in."

— Rebecca Dunham, author of *Cold Pastoral*

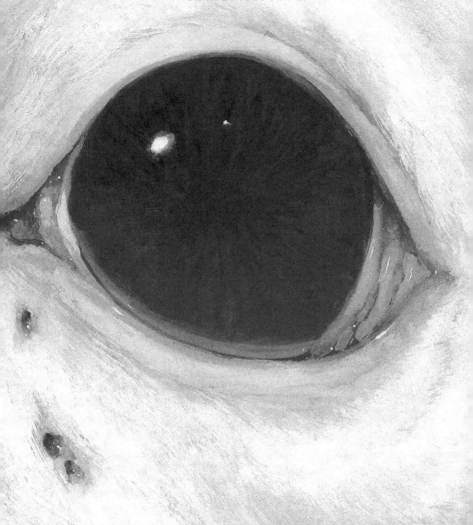

REJOICER

SKYLER OSBORNE

DRIFTWOOD
PRESS

Independently published by Driftwood Press
in the United States of America.

Managing Poetry Editor & Interviewer: Jerrod Schwarz
Poetry Editor: Andrew Hemmert
Cover Image: Dustin Ray
Cover Design: Sally Franckowiak & Jerrod Schwarz
Interior Design: Jerrod Schwarz
Copyeditor: Jerrod Schwarz
Fonts: Merriweather, Alternate Gothic No2

First published July 25th 2023
ISBN-13: 978-1-949065-27-5

Please visit our website at www.driftwoodpress.com
or email us at editor@driftwoodpress.net.

CONTENTS

I. Plains Temple

II. Glacial King

For my father

...Each leaf feels its way out,
Each a mad bible of patience.

— Larry Levis, "The Crimes of the Shade Trees"

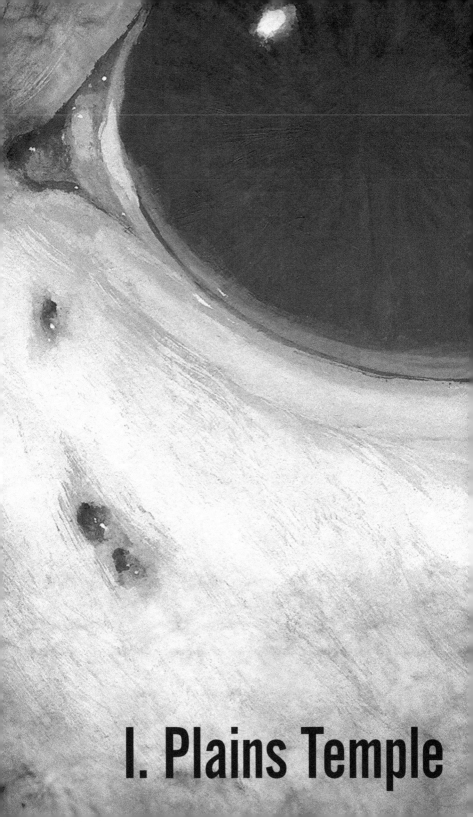

I. Plains Temple

The Magician's World

Perfect loop of the spirit
eating itself like a haunted ice cream cone—
once my grandmother opened her parasol
at the dinner table, her mind fallen out
to name her stray children. Poverty
no longer monstrous appeared
like a black tooth in bathwater.
I summoned myself to the backyard,
lobbed sharpened branches at the sky
and closed my eyes. No wonders
in that town. The train splintered the trees.
The local saints stapled roses to the barn.

A man can divide a sycamore and still love God.
A man can decapitate himself and still live
in the magician's world. Moss in my hair,
I sold old clothes and a rabbit skeleton
to the thrift center. I followed the purple blade
of light slung over the Labrador's ear,
I loved everything she loved forever.
The analog voices of the dead flared
from the radio the first time
digging a hole in the forest where I buried
a mannequin with the chest excised
and replaced by a bag of small money,
I waited for crime, somewhere
a criminal leaving hell to find it there
beneath the X and last with slow anatomy
like all the people standing in their driveways,
smoke rolling through their teeth. What a refuge.

Auras

All the swamps are flooded.
Fish swirl in choirs on the lawns.

You can come at them with a net,
a knife, a ritual, and go back to sleep.

New mountains appear this way.
The rain is driven into your hair

like a cold crown from nowhere.
My red-eyed neighbor is far off

whistling in his half-nakedness.
I worked for him, he stared through me—

orphan leaves and nicotine circling
a parallel between Nature and Progress—

the filter of the trees,
a body through a window.

My dog bit a bearded man on Thursday
because he was wrong and she was phenomenal.

When they took her, her death was golden in a room.
An ellipsis of flies blinks on and off my clothes.

Arson is brief in the trash barrels
from the defeated baseball players

thrown with refusal, all of them
leaping from their seats and crying.

The police come to spread a tape line,
a CLOSED sign over the parking lot,

and it is April everywhere.
Cicadas rhyme on the willows.

A bored girl crosses the diamond
so I remember her. I shook her hand.

She gave me peeled oranges
and a hot bird to hold.

Resplendence

Ghost-motion of the falcon over
the fanned-out palm like everything
we might kill if only our hands were larger,
the shadow left a tremor in the center of the day.

I lost my mind in brushfires, split fruits,
boredom—a brother
dragged me through some broken leaves
and beat me normal on the lawn.

Jets fleck the cirrostratus and my friends are grinning
beneath their halos. My friends
dismantle machines for money.
My friends are dazed, assassins in a graveyard.

The butterflies, wrecked and luminous,
quiver at the windows.
I am not afraid of miracles. Even now,
the skeleton. Even now, the hands.

Populations

A ship is slicing angles into the lake.
A mute is body filling a room.

There is a stone lion overlooking the beach,
litter and coins clouding his mane.

Forgive them gasping on late ice.
Forgive them, the missing.

People amble on in each ward,
linden trees hauling them down.

The coin I lost is now inside the toppled sun,
the slick little lord in my pocket on my walk

through Riverside Park. The draw
of my thought east toward the waves,

the city riots as it is pulled into rain.
Kids chime together,

shout *pop baby pop* at explosions that end
clean and cast experiments over their faces.

They come back as mist.
Tonight will take nothing—

bikes grown into fences, the houses
towered for mercy, basements

dented by names. Downtown joy
cut with sheets of trick lights,

the sky gray, then unbearable.
Throw it all to sleep.

Omens

One kidney useless,
an insect in a glass of milk,
a blot in a photograph
of snow. You walk through
the forest wall in your broken coat.

Low flashes trace the crystallized carp
in the falls. A heron is arcing off the ice
to kill something. Charcoal and small
motors reel in the scheme of winter.

Say your name. I am waiting
over words that wake up
every night glittering,
staccato with dread.

You can have my hair,
my money, my blood type.
When I pass, I will
become my body. I need
nothing to help me with my fear.

Inheritor

It was the shyness of knives begging
in the room that brought you into style.

You stole 2 apples from the market.
Green foam in your mouth and mania

blessing nothing, sunlight dancing
like a dead swan on a trampoline.

Tomorrow, a rare dog will destroy you.
An illness in the grass flushed with violets.

The old order of animals with no names
and no afterlives—

where rats living in their holes were
drowned, then shot upon surfacing.

You did that to them for money
from your father delayed with rapture.

A gang of angels straying over him
like a nerve bathed in Demerol.

His chainsaw cruising through the back
wall of the garage devoured by myth,

revulsion, stunning you breathless,
glad—the whole earth there for you

to take up: its worms and bridges.
Step over, sprint over them. Steal.

For the New Earth

Rain on the weapons. Rain
for the open mouths, a new song
dropping debt in the body.

Today, shadows.
Instructions for failure.
A lover beginning to walk through the wall.

God damn the shotgun body.
Face the moon flinching over the drowned.

      Burned barn in the center
and I hate my mistakes. I speak to a sapling,
faithlessness, the hand that put my dog to rest.

I began to live when a spider crawled through
the bricks of my dream house.

Commune

My street, my dominion,
my blue
fruit and drugs that break out of flowers—
watch me use my power
to stop these wolves from running.

The wind killed a rabbit caught in the soccer net.
I know because we watched the body hover.
But everything we planted is growing
beneath the sky stiletto and *fuck the devil*.

The light spliced through
the grass on fire
when Michael took his head,
washed his hair in the fountain.

I clapped my hands,
the crows flew out.
The face of my love met yours.

Encore

No.

The fog lifts before it reaches the bridge.

The animals will not forgive themselves for trashing the king.

I sit in bed with my teeth and limbs and brain and know
there are words without lessons.

Clarion of rain, cold language
in lieu of sedatives—

the slope of the night with a poor scrawl
and ceiling fan humming—

tiny moths
inside an ambulance.

Midwestern

If I can get calm,

throw my cash in the pond,

leave with the silhouette of my dog,

take a sword to the lawn

and flash it around

in the lonesome purposes of the day,

like the boy I knew

who would crack his own nose—

flood his shirt

to avoid the sprints

and football fields—

jam the landscape

with the shape of his body,

laugh himself still

in the mud yard,

then hold the red rag to his face

until he reappeared.

Sainted

Slow work on the 6th day,
the mouth cut out before the creation of razors.

A single body swaying in a field until it is led
elsewhere to heal over sleep like black caps of water.

It takes weeks in the kingdom to come back laughing.
I need to leave the room during silent films to throw up

because of the simulacrum.

When I broke my arm jumping off the Public Works building,
a hawk mauled the head of another hawk.

A stranger took me aside to tell me I could
meet the Lord if I loved the whole world,

even those without worship. If I helped him
and told the truth in supplication.

We used to go to church 3 times a week to howl
back at the organ. My hands were in my pockets,

or live behind the curtain where they found me sparking
matches as they walked toward me—

pink bouquets, white bouquets, singing.

Ascending

Remember the tiger standing up,
how high we were going to be?
Young magic, our heads filled with foam.
I have always ravaged the world
wanting so much
to be a part of it. To float like the vanished,
bones roaring with fiction.
When a child touches moth wings
and the gold is gone—colossal wonder
each way to fold a paper airplane,
a new word sizzles through the air.
Is that how we were made,
in the image of folding, unfolding,
blood and neon,
the slow motion of the gorgeous?
Any moment, a tree can fuck up your face.
Any moment, the smoke will meet the ocean.
I want to hang a wreath on the half-eaten
cat I found in the churchyard.
Strangers ill-starred, walk past ablaze.

Hail

You send your brother home in his tilting crown.

He walks down the driveway with steam soaring off his back.

In one photo, he is shirtless,
a gold chain racing around his neck.

I can see him about to break a bottle over his head.

Another photo is the porch
where ashes have blackened the planks.

One more is an x-ray of your father's chest
filling up with mud

at 9:38 in the morning.

Your brother was asleep in the kitchen,
his brain beaming like a car in a swimming pool.

He was an engine of blood, and parachutes were bursting in front of his f
a field where downed armies sang to him—

Hello, Moonbell.
Hello, Dreamboat.
Hello, King Shit of the World,

we're here to burn all the trees in your neighborhood.

Light after obliterated light until you stand up.

Test Clouds

Imaginary birds will begin in 5 minutes.
Dull sparkle,
a reaper in an orchard,

my black shirt changing and changing.
By my poor records,
I have stolen $40 from the now dead

without apology. I was 8 years old
when my eyes broke, when
I heard I could return as a lion.

Luno

Some dogs are speaking. Some sidereal,
dream and howl a black light.

All ascend with heroics. Those I have seen
alone in the parkway, spirits

sent forward with a crack in the pines.
The one I taught to be silent

appeared on the wall with a swerve.
I reached inside his jaws to remove a poison

he loved so terribly,
like a child held by the collar,

discovered with a face aching
in impossible thrill. There are possibilities

locked in the air, teeth
snapping at forms in the dark.

There is no distance between the Lord
and his monsters tearing up the yard.

Sermon

My body stood full
of blood at the Christmas pageant.
I spent the night awash in a man's borrowed gown

years before anyone would
tell me the northern stars are dead
and will someday eat my family.

The next week, kicked in the chest by a mare
and held accountable in the frozen barn,
chained machinery leaking oil into my hair.

I did abide in my youth, pirouette toward sugar,
and joyride at night.
I fell through the elm, wore its limbs like a king.

Alone, I asked how to touch
the many mansions rising for me,
even if a fire was there to dim its jaws on the walls.

If I stared into the flat eyes of the fish
thrashing on the ice
before I tried to gut it, alone.

Restoration

The memory arrives on the 3rd
phase of the lunar passing
and I lose my blight—
one thought
flying perpetual—one child
naming the earth with a shard of glass.

Life in the sound
and scent of the river, then the animal
corpse in the river.

This morning,
I throw rocks at the leaning wall
and wait.

Garbage Kills Bears

A razed velvet chair
and a broken door next
to the dead vegetables,
spent saline,
an empty bottle of Levothyroxine.

JESUS DOES NOT LOVE YOU
etched into the wall.

I believe another animal,
blow the blood out
of my harmonica.

I used to
feed a repulsive squirrel almonds
and avocados until it came back excellent.

I never want to see the blossoms in The Sparrow Cemetery
or hold a gone dog's full jaw.

Domain

3 horses stared at a dead horse
in the uplands. Bells

on their necks, and blood
cells in them, trillions.

Every word red automatically,
menaced by my brother,

the first crime he committed.
He will outlive the bees,

their frenzied gestures,
and drop his roses. My patriot,

devastator. My nerve disease.
If my right arm is weakened,

I will cut it off and sit
in my bankruptcy—myself

because the earth is ugly.
All of it is mine.

Late Elegy

His teeth are somewhere,

clicking like cold jars.

I have his television.

The cards are thrown through winter.

His wife's clothes are in a landfill.

Or above

a woman who loves dancing,

collects plates emblazoned with astronauts.

When my mother found a small bone

in the garden, she forgave him.

He came home from the mill

and would not die. I remembered

his last room, the bookshelf

kicked in half, as I carried him to the grave

with strangers—his chest pocket

sticky with lemon candy in heaven.

Incarnations

1.

All morning, the cypress
detonates with ugly birds.

All morning, the mud
and kicked out fires—

bodies, moths, destroyers.

2.

Fear like finding a bullet in a snowman.

3.

These are notes of praise:

A swoon from some kids in the ivy.
My knife waving from its apple.
My tongue with a slice of red half–light.

4.

I walk above this wounded spider
vibrating like a mob of drifters,
asleep and deaf to disappearing.

In the air where you have loved me

bees scatter like the Leonids
from the arms of boys
burning hives in the alley.

Animals appear
outside their vultures. Sometimes, a man
inside his worn suit is singing,
his voice twanging
like a wound through a dog. Proof

of the heavens. Lost drugs beneath
the live oak falling forward,
trash gliding in its limbs. Sometimes,
I paint a red circle and stand in the center
glowing like a drop of serotonin.

I fold a paper crane and wait for a star
to break my neck.
I beg back for your voice where you have loved me.

I will never die.

Exodus

Familiar bodies at midnight.

An arrangement of debris

after the hurricane,
my loud car.

Polaris, crushed pills.
No word, no telephone.

Gossamer hues from the lair of the moon
like a bald boy deluded in a pool.

I gathered everything to leave
in late summer,

its lunatic arms.

Alligator blood billowed
like a shirt at the bottom of the dam.

Bats sliced mosquitoes off the water.

My sister growing like a mother.

A moth glazing the back deck.

Black coffee, white pine,
last light,

rain melting on the eyes of a nurse
with full hands.

I wanted to be in love, rehearsing
hymns from my dark trumpet.

No hallelujah.
Now,

I run everywhere,
a somnambulist in a stranger's home

with a cloud in the canyon of my palm.

An apology lighting
everyone behind me.

I am living here
until I dissolve.

Blue Verse

My poor pilgrim,
I will wash your branches
and step through your blindness.

The van is blue and idle in the driveway.
Your child is growing like a bone in a hospital;
his head mastered slowly by mystics.

The enemies of forgiveness,
the enemies of empathy—what serves them?

My house is filled with gold
and milk
and morphine

and tongues
and time
and music

and berries
my oceans
and razors

and singing.
The living.

Rejoicer.

Rejoicer.

Rejoicing.

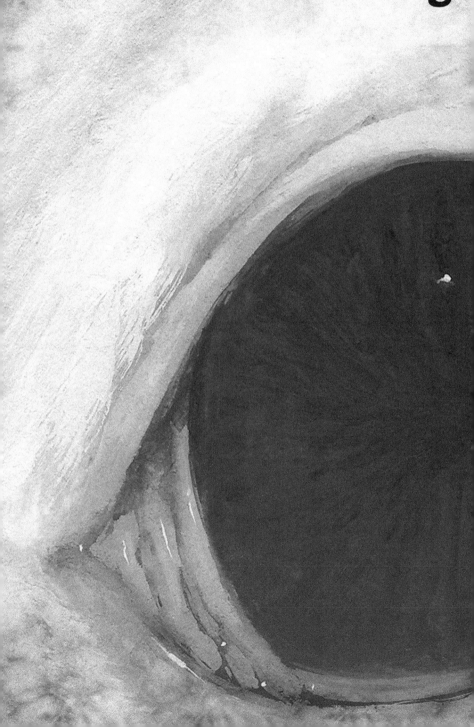

II. Glacial King

+

August 31, I refuse
to come back from the distances.
The dam breaks the southern waters.
A bone presses through the falls
like a gift.

+

My head pivots with my time in books
on language, hymns, and engines.
I will not make it to the end.

+

They called to say he was losing blood,
but he wasn't bleeding
like the horse tied to the pole,
psychotic through the fence
on the way to the abandoned schoolhouse.

I had my torch.
I touched the animal's head.
I am going to let this stand on its own
because it is bigger than me now.

UY Scuti

The vivid graveyard
of grave flowers
replaying beneath
rainbows their bloodwork,
bravado, parhelion—
a singular, ecstatic threat.
Acid from the decaying transformers
touches their veils.

There was a gothic here.
Forgotten spires.
Trees standing inside them
like they were tricked into being.

But I never stopped for the cathedral
though it led me
to the lean dog recalling
the bells that sped the ghouls
soaring out backlit,
coursing through the scene,
where the sky offers everything
to a robin living
with a hole in her spine.

Acres

I don't feel so far away.
At night, I dig a shallow pit the length of my body and lie down in it.

If the creek is dry, I hide in the 3rd chamber of the bridge and
wait for squirrels or parrots

to suddenly die from their nests on the light poles.
This is rare except when it storms.

When it does I want to
sleep in the bluebonnets and not the bent assembly of my tent.

I wrap remnants of rags around my head and imagine
trenches and comets or nothing moving at all.

I pray out loud to my mother who is kind
and alive in the country.

I let her know about the water and the food
I made for my mouth until I'm asleep.

I say, you take the soup and the bread and the meat,
hold them above the table.

I'll take the forks and the knives and the spoons
and hold them to my chest.

Yesterday, I sat in the creek bed and waited,
called my arms elegant in rain and said again,

All right, sing to whatever you're singing to today,
mother.

Summer is ash and blind and plagues of all
insects rising from deep holes in the dirt.

I fill them with fragments and shoelaces,
fire and what I can fashion with the charging grass.

I know I've made a lot of mistakes.
The animal was alive. My friends were cruel and starless.

I still dream I am in a field
digging for snakes and wringing them out in the air.

Every day I stack rocks and forgive one thing.
Every day I stack rocks and forgive one thing.

The Azimuth

Today it is not uncommon to find land mines
in our national parks.

Echoes from the North are the bravest hikers
shrieking at the sudden limbs of foxes.

I calibrate the alidade and watch smoke
arc toward the pole star.

In my tower, the sky marks a circle of my face.

Ash or snow falls slow over the country
until it shudders in the West.

The flakes abandon the higher pines.

Only insane birds.
In their throats, the dying without dying.

Spring, I ride boxcars and stalk the bombs,
unpack my instruments.

History says my family observed the sea
and kneeled at the lack of trees.

My letters on the new patterns of the wildland
will quiet The Enemy.

The photograph of the girl speaking to the headless
bear will no longer haunt the nation.

Aerology

There had been some doubt
regarding the presence of the wild gods

until the balloon met the power lines
and poured the people into the trees.

One woman was found in the basket,
in the hold of her synapses,

her eyes
like stones skipping across a pond.

In my room, I chalked the contours,
listed the marvels beyond

the point of flame.

What I read etched a meaning
in the skin of the populace.

The handsome pilot began his course,
his name littered with sleeping leaves.

Televisions had shown the branches failing.

The Thrilling of the Maples was the low song
a faraway people began to sing.

Collider

I have this vision of my friend

                              balancing an ax on his palm

            until it breaks into his head

                  and he is blind like a child is blind,

the shape of him

                              growing in the half-melted snow.

I have this vision of him.

                  He is dreaming in the backyard

                              above the latitudes

and thin hulls of insects.

                        He is under the bed with a light

            drawn to eclipse his mouth.

                        He is smiling in the dark,

a canceled city.

                  In his room, he holds

the head of an invisible animal

until I remove the cataracts from its eyes

My friend does a trick with his chest

where it blooms and serrates,

and I can tell by his face

some joy is charging through him

like a pylon, and he is the last god of his body
moving
so bright,

then violent.

Violent, then everywhere.

The Neighborhood

House of the failed doctor,
the flock of swinging girls,
the small bald king
on a slide.

House of the junk
collector whose troubled
hound groaned
above the warren.

House of the grandmother,
a woman who spilled
a circle of salt around
her husband's polished rifles.

She stood with a snake
in the waves of her floral hair.

Blaze from the cops
and the basketball court,
the crushed silver boat
like a lung in the grass.

I was an idiot child.
I flattened tomatoes,
sharpened slow arrows,
and infected the pond.

I haunted the cats.
I touched the primitive
bomb some beautiful boys
lit up in the cul-de-sac.

Dream Parade

Bewildered by the cannons
and wagon wheels,
lovesick elephants—
rifles beginning, dreamer,
over the horses' eyes—
I watched the weakest boy
lost inside the wheels
where there is no battle,
flow of marigolds,
all war when he was emptied.
The crowd took the street
like a banner over him.

There was this clairvoyance.
The blood cut from my fist
and well of my mouth,
my work made from trash
and hours, my money useless
over bridges, my mind stole
pennies from the rivers;
the bullshit crescendo
rising with the radiance
and what I will owe.

Black Fence

The rush dying in gradients
where strangers left their blankets
drawn on branches and disappeared
in murmuration
to the world again.

More for the animals
that eat the living, their joy.
R.I.P the trees
skinned with initials
and every poor motherfucker
in paradise.

For years I wore the shirt I found flying
on the wires where
the one-armed man poured liquor for his loss
and walked last unknowing
past the ruin
to meet the river,
play his punished instruments,
and touch the gray photos
in bottles near the water.

Rapture Fragment

Names of streets and songs
and the family bowing
backward until they vanished,
it all vanished.
And it estranged memory.

Here, I learned
to crack down icicles.
There, I climbed the vandal ladder
to hallucinate on the roof with a girl.
From this day forward, it is a burial.
It is all present tense.

If the rock contains pity.
That the body heals when bruised by another.
That it enters the garden to cut the garden down.
This blood is clover blood,
and the clovers are a concentration.

I don't care
if things end as they must
now, sorting through
dried mint leaves,
dead letters in my loaner coat.

The art I make is for whales sleeping vertically
in the technicolor
swarm.
It is for the list of new gods in the afterglow.

Reminder

The shark's mouth is a separate machine.
Her mind a rave
of 9,000 roses.

I look clouded through the murder of the bull.
The crests of his horns on fire—
to exit one world

and arrive in another
like something born
any second now.

You will not appear next to me
if I say your name,
though the word will come amazing.

Field Lapse

Raindrops fading on
our faces. Our pockets
replete with black seeds
and dimes when the sun launched
through the leaves. I counted
drunk wasps, carried worms
nowhere after the rain.

We had 5 apple trees
and dried blood from living.
How I could grow to hate this.
No one to forgive
the fleck of light on the red hand
above the dog
where she was harbored.

I kept rising from the woodpile.
I was not surprised I was
holding the fuel and my head,
the hatchet—the forest abysmal
because we pointed, we worked,
and the theme forever became
destruction. I said,

Lord, help my mother. Lord,
complete the circle.
Don't bring us back.
Lord, flip the coin.

Aubade

The grass burned back.
A quilt with one black square.

Of course, we were always
made of dirt and flags.
Of course, the dog eats the wall
when you leave it alone.

The sun is pouring fractals.
Reprise, the stilled pastures.

Embrace

Drawing closer to the rage
growing in the grove, still
green-weaved, waking to bear it,
I kicked the low trees,
ate the ice falling from them
when they lifted. The creek-black fish
practiced the shadows nonetheless,
bliss dreamless and thoughtless,
riding satin like a scar
when I was young and would not
bury the velocity. The moth
dissolved on the wall until spectral.
The frozen cardinal I found was the oracle
and blood gift repeating the joy
that spread through us. The blossoms
on the hill, ungraying, slanted back hello—
snow-dusted corpse without loneliness.

Fletching

In the same clothes as yesterday,
and my voice
cylindrical
like an echo
populating
a friend,
I speak into my hands,
stall over the sidewalks,
leave the whirring
in the deadfall—
an angel
cashed-out in the evergreen—
an astonished child
spreading the wings
with a stick.

An Unkindness of Ravens

Born poor, then made
poorer by my ugliness
and the drafts of winter.

My lies like pigs with demolished heads.

Quietness coming off the grasses
where I want to be found
buried beneath my three charms:

the rusted necklace,
the pressed chrysanthemum,
the kidney stone from the circus clown,

then all the money I am owed for my birthdays—

before the day comes
when my hatred bends from the mountain
to pick up its ridiculous hat.

Higher

I watched a man eat a dove.
It meant nothing. Somewhere

he is sleeping and will soon fossilize
like all the children of God. I want to rise

from that meridian completely outraged.
My face brightens and declines continuously.

Everything I've read has made me
rich and disgusting with joy.

The raptors where we play
land and defecate on the cross.

Nothing in the world with purpose,
nothing symbolic.

No devotion to this kingdom—
lake ice to bleed on.

I run, a beggar in a golden circle,
trying a new music with my hands.

The cosmic hole inside
each animal is filling with snow.

Petals

A litany of beleaguered hogs
one day drifted through here
dazzling everyone like pornography
in a strawberry field.
They stole a woman's shoes
and assembled to the far
trees—a mouth
solving a green equation.

A mass of insomniacs doze in the shade
and no one speaks to them.
Flowers accelerate over the faded.
I am pretending
I am responsible
for this. I look over
my shoulder at the man
with half a face dropping
the alphabet into the jade.
The petals add to him.

Zooscopy

2,000,000 bats
stain the facsimiles of faces,
filthy words seared on the estuary wall
where I lost: 11 dollars,
a full bottle of amber venom,
a leather journal riddled with language,
and various shouts at phantoms.
No other complications strike me.
Look, the whole universe wants to
fuck the wildflowers.
Look at the practice of mathematics
inside the borders of the astrobleme.
Desert populations swallow air
and scare each shape from the witch grass.
They point to astral traces until they die
on the hoods of rusted cars.
Sad plants diminish into wire.
Children fall out of their bodies, graze
their eyelids on the lithe ribs of geckos.
Each new thought like retrieving
a severed limb from the top of the monolith,
they decide to live and move
so far from pain. Thunderheads
multiply and kill each other. Look,
an eagle is chewing a frog in the baffled rain.

Flood Pastoral

Where the state used to be ocean,
we held up shells
drafted in cold springs,
new water.

We were hiking the rock bed
reciting, *the horse trainer's cabin.*
The horses like a sonnet
in their reins and class and muscle.

14 of them drowned
with the bending of the cypresses,
dragged out of the subdivisions
by difficult trucks.

We died in this house until it was gone.

Gulls transpose our faces,
sprawl through picnics,
eat paper and green
pennies in the peak
of the 100-year floodplain.

Once or twice a year,
the land is cut in half.

Faster when the stars arrive
immolated like sugar
in a bloodstream. On a normal day,
I can swim to the rocks on either side,
the current
blaming the limestone.

Today, I wanted to touch one of the coyotes
I watched scavenge the campsite.

Last year, the Halloween floods
at Arrow Creek, near its mouth.

Smoking, No Hands

Now there is nothing to do

but talk to your god in the distance

like a sail dropping before a mirror.

Debris over the ocean.

Slow ode to heaven.

Here is a fist around a snake until it vomits

what it has taken.

Signal of red dripping down

a fang,

born into everything,

bright on your clothes.

Enfolding

Ghost hazing the floor,
having resolved each wall and window,
its presence hurled deer through the door—
it would not speak to me.

Doctors were disillusioned,
ashes smoldered on their wrists.
Passersby became huge with loneliness.

The neighbors continued to thrive
and mow their lawns in contours
despite wasps drilling the walls,
a few alive at night on the beds.
Their sheds and homes fumed
with poisons that pulled water
out of the frame in whorls.
A fugue in the lungs made them
incandescent, and there was always this
slime from the births of rodents
slung in the cream red reeds.

Ghost like nothing
radiating my face. I spoke
a perfect consonant, filled the scene
with garbage, dragged the heartbeat
around like an anchor.

If I leaped into the chasm
driven through the center of the world,
it would take me
42 minutes to appear dead
and famous on the other side.

Deconstructed Owl

Bright men sprinting near Sugar River
pulse in their distortion.
They drift away from me like sobriety.
The bird out here spins
her face in a flare.

Yes, it gets darker
where one hand touches another.
I lived in ceremony,
it did not change me.
I tried to give it all away
in the water behind us.

Forgive yourself,
your disillusions,
and the range of your tenderness.
Keep me from growing pathetically.
I do not want to kill.
I want to remain on Earth
where there is purple flourishing,
moss overthrowing.
The voice at night says cherry
over the sound of the blackout
fragments of trains.

For the Old Earth

When I reached for the damaged crow
trapped in the hole of the tire swing,

the field deleted,

    the vespiary filled.

Blank face on the last person to touch my chest.

Atrophy, the sound ice carries over a sea when it is warming.

    I had asked for a life with a joke at the end.

Islands break off.
    Murmur total loss.

Passage

On the riverbank, an old couch is steaming
like a horse asleep in winter.

Everything that is dead was once filled with water.
The world

shimmering,
a gash in the solar plexus.

The world of bodies
crumbling over one another in the light.

The nerves like a string breezing,

breezing,
breaking the legs
together for song.

The world without.

Say it.

A child will pull it apart.
A child will eat it,
piece by piece.

Strobe

You are the ultramarine thing

beheading my friends in the gymnasium.

Cold glow flying through the silk

film of the dilated eye in paradise.

The zero appeared on the forehead.

A slash on the cheek

from the curve of the earth.

Parachutes, crates of pears,

and a whole boy with an oar

inside my monster consciousness.

The city where I am to be

burned but will not drop

the soaking wet blanket.

At the end of the rainbow:

clear water, delirium.

At the end of suffering,

a stillborn star.

Snowfall, finally.

Snowfall, here.

Everyone aghast in their gardens.

AN ECSTATIC THREAT AGAINST EVERYTHING

A Conversation with Skyler Osborne & Jerrod Schwarz

Skyler, what a joy it's been to read and publish REJOICER! It's a phenomenal collection of poems, and I can't wait to learn more about your process and the work that went into your writing. I want to open our interview with a discussion of one of the books larger concerns: place and geography. Which settings and locations influenced these poems the most?

Midwestern America. Most of the poems are written from an adult perspective, but they're strained by the forests and plains where I lived for the first half of my childhood. It was natural then and real, but it's an imaginative and meditative space now: a field behind my family's first home where I would lay face up, the breeze kicking through the tall grass. In a sense, I'm always living there, alone when I start to write. That's really how I think of it.

Later, we moved to a small town, and the scenery changed, but it was a similar spirit. The alleys and neighborhoods, strangers' lives, streets with their mythical trash, all the yards full of possibilities.

I go on walks in these settings when I'm having trouble finding what a particular poem wants. I tend to pick up stray sticks and break them into pieces as I go on ruminating, looking for an image, or waiting for something to strike me. I became aware of this habit early in the process, and I realized the manuscript was about how I was affecting the world as I raged through it.

It's so interesting that rage exists as the onus of these poems. As a reader, REJOICER felt like sneaking up on the aftermath of a wreck; I felt witness to the limp, not the break. Reflecting on your collection after-the-fact, what do you think that rage turned into?

Sorting through destruction and wreckage, living in and with it, yes: those themes are constant. At times, I feel like I wrote during a blackout. The rage there is more so a kind of intensity—rebellion, a cosmic and therefore incomprehensible violence—an ardent reaction. Of course, there is physical anger as well, but I can't give in to that if I want to survive.

Looking back, I believe that rage grew into shock, astonishment, then resignation. If the sky is falling, how will we interpret it? How will we greet it?

Let's dive into the visual language of the collection. These poems are often terse, single-page works with short line lengths. Is this how your poems usually present themselves, or is the visual language here unique to REJOICER? Additionally, what did the first drafts of these poems look like?

Yes, I like to get in and get the hell out. This is true of everything I do. It wasn't always true of poetry, however. Early on, I was writing these lofty, sort of romantic poems, and they were landing well enough, but I fell out of that style quickly because I couldn't believe myself.

The poems I love are magic tricks. Card tricks. They move like them. Each word, each line is shocking and carries weight—they devastate you quickly. They're loaded with mystery and maybe you feel them before you comprehend them. I think in images. I first see each poem almost as a film played out. I can't really explain it, and I like it that way. I've settled now without much explanation. It happened around the time I started REJOICER, so the poems looked much the same in early drafts. My work is still appearing in that terse, compact way.

Sleight-of-hand is such a fantastic way of describing the visual language (and syntax) in this collection. I think a lot of what I love in these poems boils down to trusting the reader and, more specifically, allowing the reader agency of interpretation. When you are drafting poems, do you think about audience? Or, do you think about the reader at all?

Honestly, I'm too caught up—I don't think much about how a particular reader will access the work. I write alone and for the spirit of it. I present the scene and let the feeling of the poem sort out the guesswork. Maybe this sounds unhinged...when a poem is really working you feel it in your throat or chest. Whatever that sensation is, if it's not there, I know I need to keep digging. I do at least hope readers perceive a visceral intensity, and that exhilaration often contextualizes the work.

Investigations into spirituality are the crux of these poems. Perhaps more specifically, REJOICER is deeply concerned with the rituals that mankind uses to express spiritual truths. As a poet, what are the challenges and joys in writing about ritual and belief?

It's complex and fragile, and I only want to speak to the joy in it, which has been the permission to write my way towards what I consider spiritual, what I have to believe and strive for to outlast consciousness.

How can I forgive myself in this life and for this world? And what will become of us? I want to know if some part of me will survive this earth, so I look to poetry as a ritual itself and vessel for forgiveness. I wrote the book and titled it the way I did as a form of resistance. It is an ecstatic threat against everything.

It's one of my favorite collection titles, and the poems within are a testament to that forgiveness. Do you think you will return to these themes in future work, or does REJOICER feel contained? What are you working on currently?

I won't escape those themes. They have taken root. But now I can say I'm charged more by harmony than dissonance and I move to forgiveness with a greater defiance and urgency. So, I don't believe REJOICER is contained, I think it is only beginning.

I'm working on the foundation of a second collection. Fragments. That's just my method—I don't force it. But I am finally aware. I'm sensing a vibrancy and reality that excites me.

What media outside of poetry inspires you?

Music and film and fiction and fire. All styles and approaches. But I'm constantly surprised by music. Of course, all poetry has a sonic ecosystem. I'm attracted to lyrical depth and sensitive instrumentation or, conversely, something totally vicious: music that explodes and throws landscapes of sound. REJOICER and most of my work is built with a mind in both of those worlds.

Are there any poets or books that felt like seminal inspiration when writing REJOICER?

Not exactly. I'm always trying to build a literary foundation. As I wrote, I learned I had to fall into love with all poetry and radical wisdom. I read too many books to name. Mostly those written in the current or previous century. I did read quite a few first books and early poems, and I read widely and spasmodically until I wasn't reading at all, which I found wildly disturbing and compelling.

What advice would you give to other poets looking to complete a full-length manuscript? If you could speak to your younger poet-self, what would you say?

You'll gain the most traction alternatively and through lived experience. Safeguard your imagination. Energize it. Writing can be pretty fucking annoying and it can be boring to talk about. So, escape instances that stress your spirit, and avoid ideas that complicate your specific process. And that process will develop with time and patience. Sounds simple enough, but you'll be surprised at what you'll have to endure. I would say the same things to my younger self. He was and still is very nervous about these things. It's delusional pressure. You are in charge of your study, your art, your time, your joy.

ACKNOWLEDGEMENTS

"The Magician's World," *Best New Poets*, 2019

"For the New Earth" and "Higher," *Birdcoat Quarterly*, 2022

"Inheritor," *Blue Earth Review*, 2021

"Sermon," *The Boiler Journal*, 2020

"In the air where you have loved me," *The Colorado Review*, 2019

"Blue Verse," *Driftwood Press*, 2023

"Resplendence," *fields magazine*, 2018

"An Unkindness of Ravens," *The Greensboro Review*, 2022

"Domain" and "Exodus," *The Meadow*, 2021

"Incarnations," *Narrative Magazine*, 2017

"The Neighborhood," *Ninth Letter*, 2021

"The Magician's World," *No Tokens*, 2019

"Midwestern," *River, River*, 2018

"Populations" and "Acres," *Salt Hill*, 2020

"Passage," *Seneca Review*, 2023

"Garbage Kills Bears," *Burnside Review*, 2023

THANKS

My thanks to the editors of the following journals in which these poems first appeared: *Best New Poets, Birdcoat Quarterly, Blue Earth Review, The Boiler Journal, Burnside Review, The Colorado Review, Driftwood Press, fields, The Greensboro Review, The Meadow, Narrative Magazine, Ninth Letter, No Tokens, River River, Salt Hill,* and *Seneca Review.*

Thank you to the James A. Michener Center at the University of Texas at Austin for the time and support.

Special thanks to Rebecca Dunham, Michael McGriff, Jane Miller, and Kevin Prufer.

Endless love to my family and animals, my friends, teachers, and contributors.

Dad, thank you for showing me this world.

Sam, my everything. I will always dream of you.

Luno and Henry, my boys for life, be brave.

Nick Almeida, your encouragement and laughter have carried me.

To the memory and generosity of Dean Young.

My final debt to James McNulty, Jerrod Schwarz, and everyone at *Driftwood Press* for their fearless dedication to art and imagination.

photo by James Cassidy

Skyler Osborne was born and raised in the Midwest. He received an MFA in Writing from the Michener Center for Writers at the University of Texas at Austin. His work has appeared in *Best New Poets*, *The Colorado Review*, *The Greensboro Review*, and *Salt Hill*, among other publications.